jK

Looking at Stars

Night Sky

Robin Kerrod

Thameside Press

Distributed in the United States by
Smart Apple Media
1980 Lookout Drive
North Mankato, MN 56003

Text copyright © by Robin Kerrod 2001

Editor: Veronica Ross
Designer: Helen James
Illustrator: Chris Forsey
Consultant: Doug Millard
Picture researcher: Diana Morris

Printed in Hong Kong

Library of Congress Cataloging-in-Publication Data

Kerrod, Robin.
  Night Sky / written by Robin Kerrod.
    p. cm. -- (Looking at stars)
  Includes index.
  Summary: Describes what stars and constellations can be seen in the night sky and
provides instructions for finding them.
    ISBN 1-930643-25-X
    1. Astronomy--Observers' manuals—Juvenile literature. [1. Astronomy--Observers'
manuals.] I. Title.

  QB63 .K44 2001
  523.8'022'3--dc21   2001027277

9 8 7 6 5 4 3 2 1

Photo credits
Robin Kerrod: 1, 14cl, 15bl, 18bl.
Lick Observatory, © UC Regents: 13cr.
Rob Matheson/Stockmarket/Corbis: 5c.
NASA/Spacecharts: 15br,
Royal Astronomical Society/Spacecharts: 10tl, 13bl.
Spacecharts: front cover, 7tr, 8bl, 8-9c, 9t, 9b, 11t, 11b, 13tl, 14br, 17c, 17b, 19tr, 21t.
Science & Society Picture Library: 17t.

Contents

Introducing the night sky

On every clear night, nature puts on a spectacular show— the starry sky. Thousands and thousands of **stars** shine down on our world out of the blackness that is space. They twinkle and sparkle like jewels scattered on black velvet. We often call the starry sky, the **heavens**,

The heavens are full of other delights besides the stars. The silvery Moon appears most nights, shining brilliantly. Some stars seem to wander around the sky. Others seem to be falling to Earth. Sometimes, what look like big stars with long, flowing tails come into view.

Starting stargazing

Every night, millions of people look up at the night sky to see what is happening. Stargazing is one of the world's most popular pastimes. Scientists who study the night sky are called **astronomers**.

To begin stargazing, you need no equipment at all—just your eyes. Go somewhere that is very dark, away from the glare of street lights and car headlights. Always go with an adult you know. Let your eyes get used to the dark before you start stargazing.

▽ **Wrapping up**
On cold nights wear a thick sweater, jacket, scarf, and woolly gloves. Thick socks and boots will keep your feet warm.

◁ **Star guide**
Using a planisphere like this, you can find which stars are on view on every night of the year.

▷ Trailing stars

You can take pictures of the night sky even with a simple camera. The stars make trails like this.

▽ Some like it hot

A hot chocolate or other drink will help keep out the cold. A snack also goes down well!

◁ Jot it down

Take a notebook and pencil to jot down notes about what you see and when.

Winter skies

The stars look brightest on cold, clear nights. Winter skies are best. A few pieces of equipment will help you get the most out of stargazing. Star maps and a planisphere will help you find your way around the sky. With a pair of binoculars, the heavens look even more spectacular.

Stars in your eyes

The night sky is full of stars. Just using our eyes, we can see more than 2,500 of them. Through binoculars, we can see thousands more. Through **telescopes**, astronomers can see millions upon millions.

When you first look at the sky, it seems to be the same everywhere. But if you look closely, you see that various parts of the sky look different.

△ Beacon stars
Some stars stand out like beacons in the sky. The brightest star here is named Deneb.

△ The Milky Way
*A faint milk-white band of light arches across the night sky. We call it the **Milky Way**.*

◁ **Sparkling like jewels**
*In some parts of the heavens,
stars cluster together.*

Bright stars

Some parts of the sky
have more stars than others.
The stars are different, too.
Some shine brightly like beacons,
while others glow feebly like glowworms.
Some stars are a brilliant blue-white,
while others are yellow, orange, or
red. Most stars appear on their own,
but some have companions. A few
group together in clusters.

▽ **Colorful clouds**
*In places, great glowing clouds
of gas and dust appear
among the stars.
These are called
nebulas.*

9

◁ Orion in the night sky
Orion is a bright constellation and is easy to spot.

△ Linking the stars
Linking up the bright stars in Orion gives us a pattern like this.

Patterns in the sky

The first thing you need to do when you go stargazing is to find your way about the sky. Look at the sky for a while. Some stars are brighter than others. In your imagination, try to join these stars together to form patterns. Look for these same patterns the next time you go stargazing. When you see them, you are beginning to find your way around the night sky. We call the patterns the stars make the **constellations**.

Flying swans

Ancient astronomers saw the same constellations as we do today. They named the constellations after figures they thought the star patterns looked like.

For example, one star pattern looks like a flying swan; another is like a scorpion with its curved tail ready to sting. Here is a hunter, and there are twin boys. Only a few of the constellations really look like the figures they are named after.

△ **The mighty hunter**
Ancient astronomers pictured Orion as a hunter. He has a club in his right hand, ready to strike a blow.

▷ **Fanciful figures**
Heroes and heroines, beasts, and birds appear in this ancient map of constellations.

Queen of the night

The Moon circles the Earth once a month. It does not give out any light of its own. We see it shine because it is lit by the Sun.

But the Moon does not stay the same every night. On some nights, we see it as a thin curve, or crescent. On others, it appears to be a full circle. On some nights, we can't see it at all.

The Moon appears to change shape because different amounts of it are lit up by the Sun each night. These shapes are called the **phases of the Moon.**

Turning round

These pictures show different phases of the Moon. To get the right view, you need to turn the book around. Begin by turning it to the right so that "1 New Moon" appears the right-way up.

△ 1 New Moon

At the start of each month, we can't see the Moon. This is called a New Moon. The Sun lights up the Moon's far side. The near side, the side that faces us, is in darkness.

(Turn the book to the right.)*

◁ 4 Last quarter

After another week, the Moon again appears as a half-circle. We call this the Last quarter. The Sun now lights up only the left-hand side of the Moon. Over the next week, the lit-up area shrinks until it disappears completely at the next New Moon.

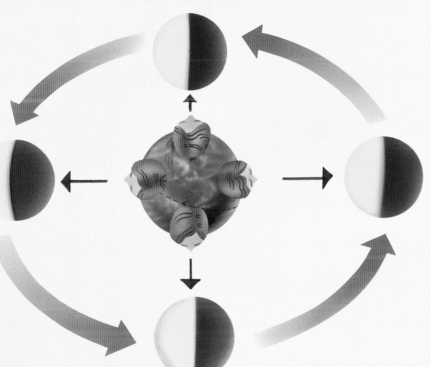

△ 3 Full Moon

After another week, the Moon appears as a full circle. We call it a Full Moon. The Sun is behind us and lights up the whole of the near side of the Moon. Now the far side is dark. (Turn the book to the right.)

Stars that wander

On some evenings, just after the Sun has set, a bright star appears in the sky. No other stars are out yet. We call this bright star the evening star. But the evening star is not a star at all. It is a **planet**. A star is a great ball of very hot gas like the Sun. But the evening star is a ball of rock, like the Earth.

▽ Rocky planet

Venus is covered with huge volcanoes.

△ Evening star

The evening star, Venus, and a crescent Moon appear together at sunset.

Circling in space

The evening star is the planet Venus. It is one of five planets we can see in the sky. The other planets we can see are Mercury, Mars, Jupiter, and Saturn. Mercury and Mars are rocky planets like Venus. But Jupiter and Saturn are great balls of cold gas and liquid.

The word planet means wanderer, because planets look like stars that wander across the sky.

The Earth is also a planet. Another three planets, Uranus, Neptune, and Pluto, are too far away to be seen. All the planets, including the Earth, circle in space around the Sun.

▽ **Great gas ball**
Seen close-up, giant Jupiter is covered with bands of colored clouds.

▽ **Bright shiners**
Mars (left) and Jupiter shine brightly in the evening sky.

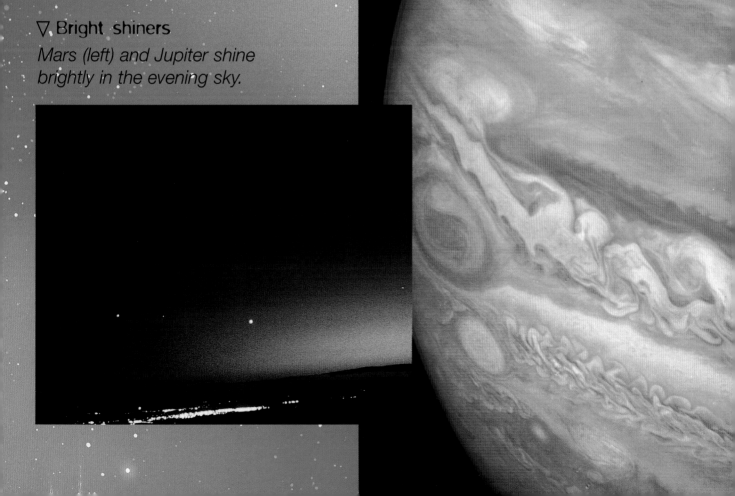

Catch a falling star

When you go stargazing, you will almost always see bright streaks in the sky. It looks as if some of the stars are dropping out of the heavens or shooting off to a different constellation. We call these streaks falling stars or **shooting stars.**

But stars don't fall from the sky or move around. The streaks are made by specks of rock from outer space traveling through the air high above the Earth. They are called **meteors**.

▷ **It's raining meteors**
Specks and lumps from outer space rain down on the Earth all the time. Most burn up in the air, but some reach the ground and dig out craters.

▷ **Metal meteorite**

This meteorite is made up of metals, mainly iron and nickel. But most meteorites are made up of rock.

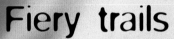

▷ **What a shower**

Two meteors flash by during a meteor shower. In a shower, many more meteors occur than usual.

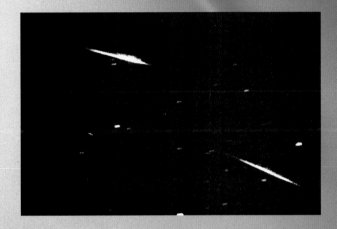

Fiery trails

As the specks of rock hit the air, they heat up and catch fire. They leave behind a fiery trail that we see as a meteor.

Sometimes bigger lumps of rock don't completely burn up. Some bits fall down and hit the Earth. We call them meteorites.

Big meteorites hit the ground very hard and dig out craters. If a big meteorite crashed into a city, it would knock down buildings and kill many people.

▷ **Meteor crater**

About 50,000 years ago, a big meteorite dug out this huge crater in Arizona. It is more than 3/4 mile (1200 metres) across.

Stars with tails

Comets are the most spectacular of the heavenly bodies. They can shine more brightly than the brightest stars. And their tails can stretch for millions of miles (kilometers).

Comets circle the Sun, just like the planets. But they can take thousands of years to make the journey. Usually we don't know when they are going to appear in the sky.

Long ago, people were afraid when a comet appeared. They thought it would cause disasters and wars. A comet appeared at the Battle of Hastings in 1066, when the English King Harold was killed.

The 1066 comet has been seen many times. It is named Halley's comet after the English astronomer Edmond Halley. It last appeared in 1986, and should return in 2062.

◁ The comet of 1997
This comet was named Hale-Bopp after the two astronomers who discovered it. It was one of the brightest comets of recent years.

Jets of gas shoot out of the body of Halley's comet. A spacecraft called Giotto took this picture in 1986.

Ice and dust

Comets are often called dirty snowballs because they are made up of ice and dust. Most of the time they are frozen solid. But they start to melt when they are near the Sun. Then they give off clouds of gas and dust that shine in the sunlight.

△ Heads and tails

The brightest part of a comet is the head. One or two tails grow out from the head as the comet gets nearer the Sun.

The heavens above

When we look up at the night sky, it seems like a great dark bowl over our heads. It is the same wherever we go on Earth.

Ancient astronomers believed that the Earth lay inside a dark ball, or sphere. They called it the **celestial** (heavenly) **sphere**. They thought that the stars were stuck on the inside of the sphere. They could see that the sphere spun round, and they believed that this made the stars move across the sky during the night.

We now know that there is no such thing as a celestial sphere. The stars are scattered at different distances throughout space. And the stars move across the night sky because the Earth is spinning round.

Horizon

◁ **The sky dome**
Everywhere you go, the sky seems to form a huge bowl over your head. The bowl meets the ground in the distance, on the horizon.

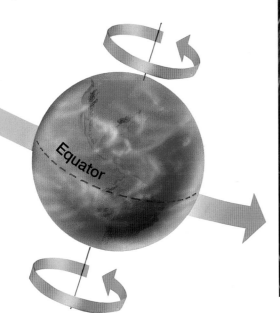

△ Spinning round

The Earth spins round in space once a day.

△ Star trails

The spinning of the Earth makes the stars appear to whirl around at night.

▷ The celestial sphere

Astronomers once thought that the stars were stuck to the inside of a sphere that spins around the Earth. We can think of it in two halves, called the northern and southern hemispheres.

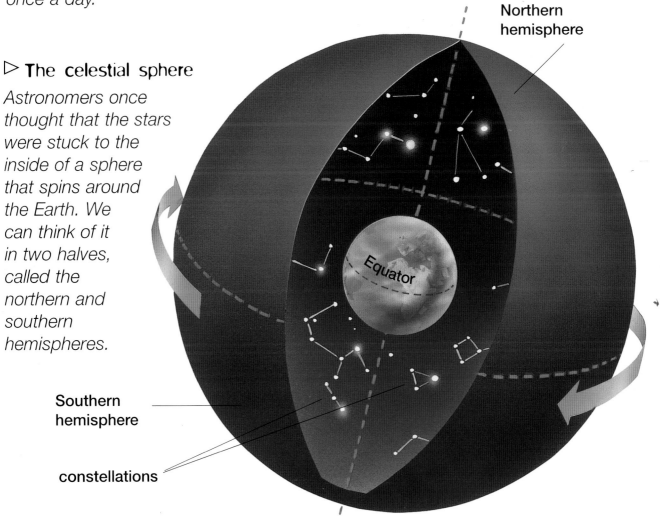

Northern hemisphere

Southern hemisphere

constellations

Constellations north and south

Here are the main star patterns, or constellations, that we can see in the two hemispheres (halves) of the night sky. We show just a few bright stars for each constellation.

Northern hemisphere

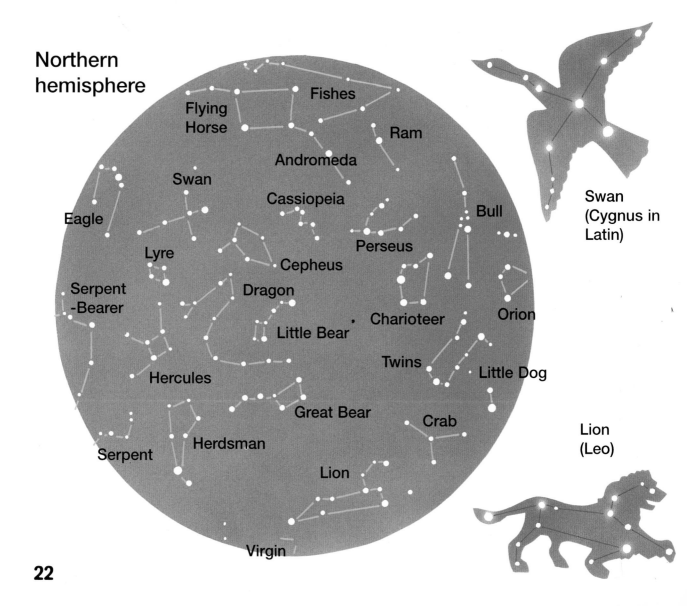

Fishes
Flying Horse
Ram
Andromeda
Swan
Cassiopeia
Bull
Eagle
Perseus
Lyre
Cepheus
Serpent-Bearer
Dragon
Charioteer
Orion
Little Bear
Twins
Little Dog
Hercules
Great Bear
Crab
Serpent
Herdsman
Lion
Virgin

Swan (Cygnus in Latin)

Lion (Leo)

The names of the constellations are given in English. Astronomers give them Latin names.

Southern hemisphere

Scorpion (Scorpius)

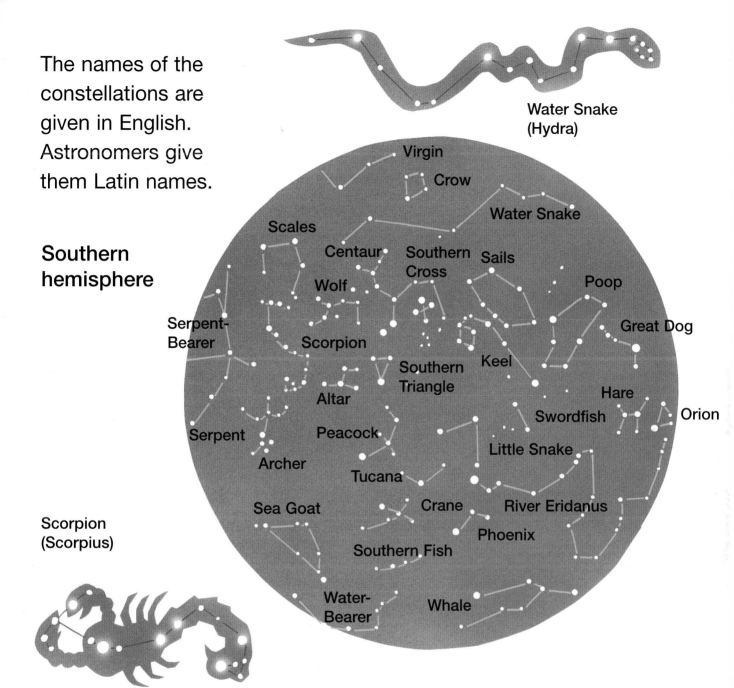

Water Snake (Hydra)

Virgin

Crow

Water Snake

Scales

Centaur

Southern Cross

Sails

Poop

Wolf

Serpent-Bearer

Scorpion

Great Dog

Southern Triangle

Keel

Hare

Altar

Swordfish

Orion

Serpent

Peacock

Little Snake

Archer

Tucana

Sea Goat

Crane

River Eridanus

Phoenix

Southern Fish

Water-Bearer

Whale

Seeing stars

Which constellations you see during the year depends on where in the world you live. From most places, you will see some of the constellations of the northern hemisphere and some of the southern hemisphere. But there are some constellations that you never see. They are seen from the other side of the Earth.

Now you see them

The night sky never stays the same. It changes hour by hour during the night. And it also changes month by month and season by season.

When you stargaze for a long time, you notice that the constellations slowly move across the sky. This happens because the Earth spins round in space once a day.

The Earth spins round from west to east. This makes the stars move in the opposite direction, from east to west. This is the same direction in which the Sun travels across the sky during the daytime.

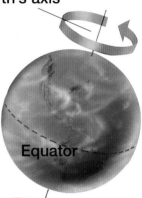

Earth's axis

▷ Spinning
The Earth spins on its axis.

Equator

◁ Rising and setting
The stars rise in the east when it gets dark. They climb to their highest point in the south. Then they set in the west when daylight comes again.

Eastern horizon

North

South

Western horizon

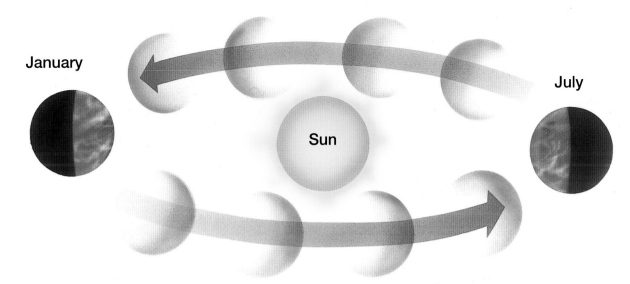

January

Sun

July

Because the stars are always moving, they lie in different directions in the sky at different times. This is why a time (10:30 P.M.) is given with the star maps that follow. The maps show the positions of the constellations at that time.

As the months go by, some constellations disappear and others take their place. The constellations change because the Earth circles around the Sun during the year.

△ **Circling the Sun**
In January and July, the Earth lies on opposite sides of the Sun.

▽ **Changing skies**
In January, the night side of the Earth looks out on to one part of the heavens. In July, it looks out on to the other part. This is why we see different constellations during these months.

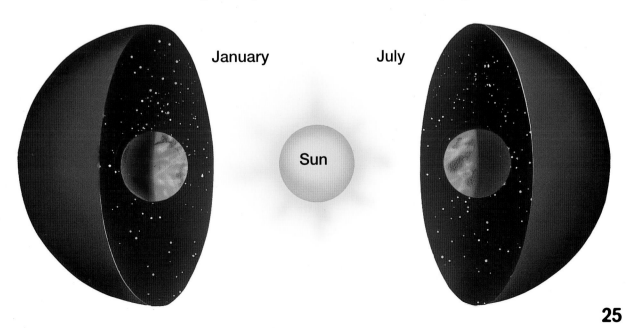

January

July

Sun

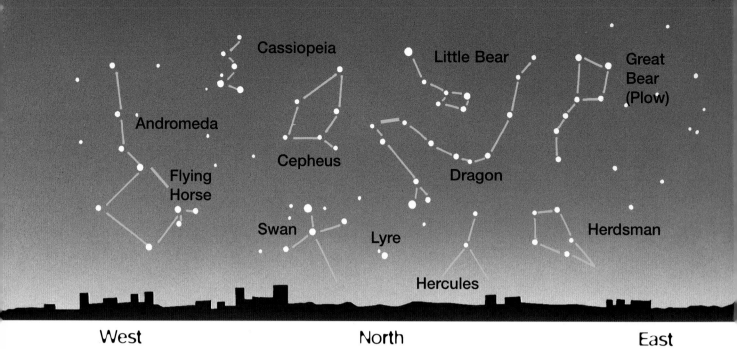

West — North — East

January skies

The maps on these pages show the stars you can see early in January. You see different constellations in different parts of the world. In northern parts it is winter. In southern parts it is summer.

△ **Europe, North America**
Looking north at about 10:30 P.M. in the first week in January.

▽ **Australia, South America**
Looking north at about 10:30 P.M. in the first week in January.

West — North — East

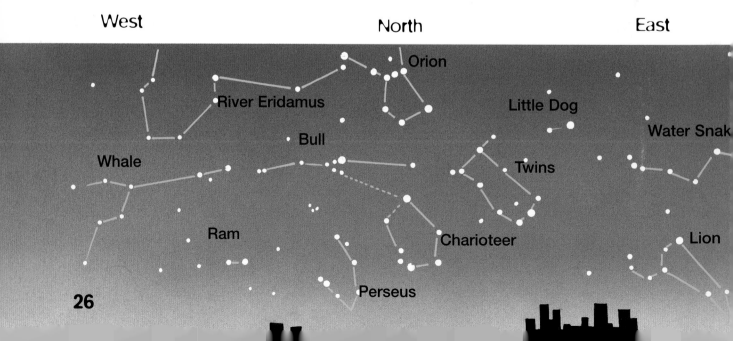

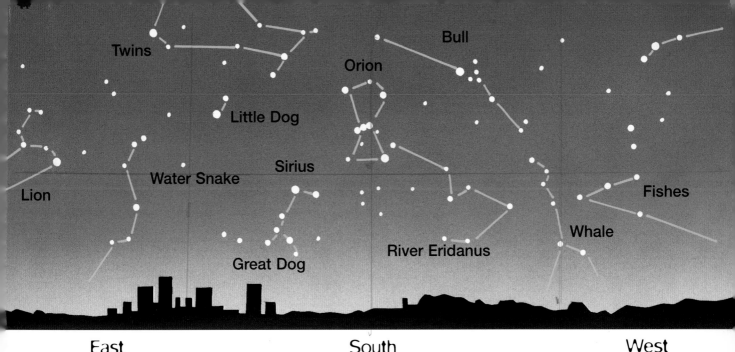

East	South	West

In northern parts looking north, the easiest stars to spot are the Plow and Cassiopeia. Looking south, you can't miss Orion and the very bright star Sirius.

△ **Europe, North America**

Looking south at about 10:30 P.M. in the first week in January.

In southern parts, you find Orion when you look north, with the Bull (Taurus) and the Twins (Gemini) nearby. Looking south, you can't mistake the Southern Cross (Crux).

▽ **Australia, South America**

Looking south at about 10:30 P.M. in the first week in January.

East	South	West

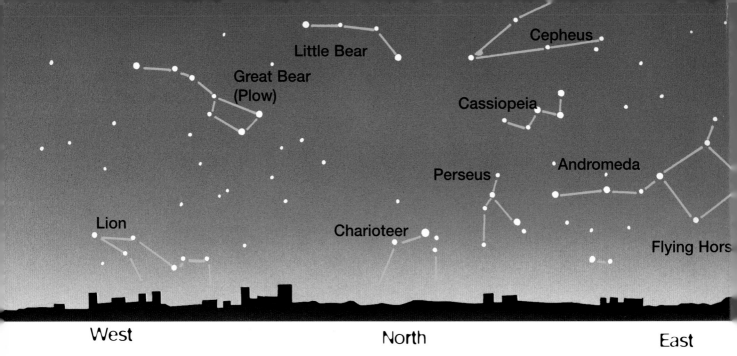

West North East

July skies

Here are the constellations you can see early in July. Now it is summer in northern parts of the world, and winter in southern parts. Many new constellations have come into view. Others have moved.

△ **Europe, North America**
Looking north at about 10:30 P.M. in the first week in July.

▽ **Australia, South America**
Looking north at about 10:30 P.M. in the first week in July.

West North East

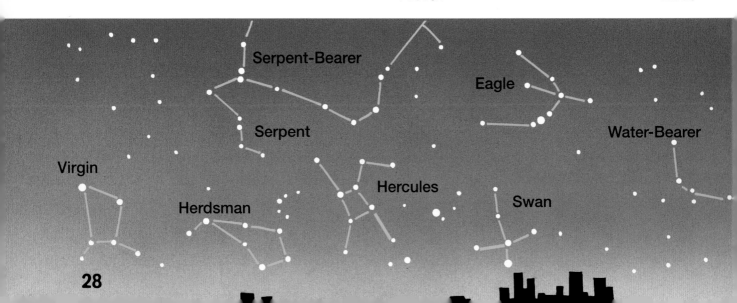

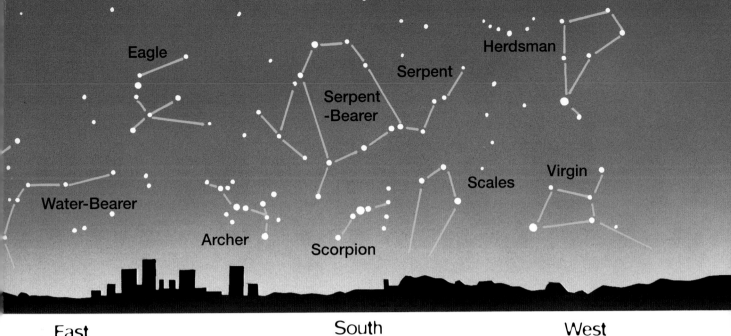

East   South   West

In northern parts looking north, the Plow and Cassiopeia have swapped places. Looking south, Orion has disappeared. The Eagle (Aquila) is easiest to spot.

In southern parts, the Eagle is found looking north, with the Swan (Cygnus) nearby. Looking south, the Southern Cross is now on the other side of the sky.

△ Europe, North America

Looking south at about 10:30 P.M. in the first week in July.

▽ Australia, South America

Looking south at about 10:30 P.M. in the first week in July.

East   South   West

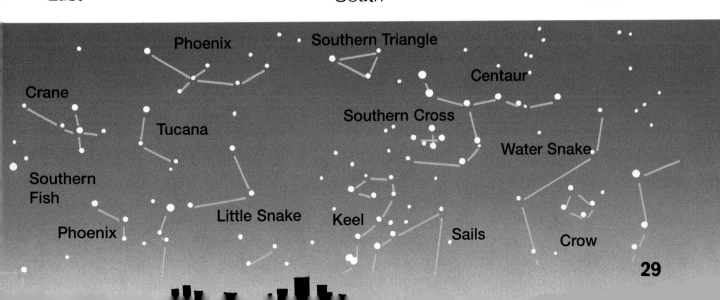

Written in the stars

During the year, the Earth circles the Sun. But, seen from the Earth, the Sun seems to move among the stars. Every month it travels through one of the constellations. All the planets travel through these same 12 constellations, too.

These constellations are known as the constellations of the zodiac. The word zodiac means "circle of animals." This is because most of the constellations are named after animals, such as Aries (the Ram) and Pisces (the Fishes).

People once thought that the constellations of the zodiac must be very special. They believed that these stars somehow affected what they were like and what happened to them. Even today, some people think that the stars affect their lives. This idea is called **astrology**.

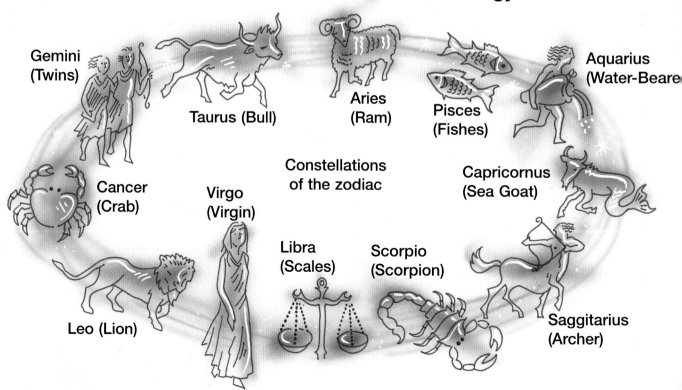

Gemini (Twins)

Taurus (Bull)

Aries (Ram)

Pisces (Fishes)

Aquarius (Water-Beare

Cancer (Crab)

Virgo (Virgin)

Constellations of the zodiac

Capricornus (Sea Goat)

Leo (Lion)

Libra (Scales)

Scorpio (Scorpion)

Saggitarius (Archer)

Useful words

astrology   The idea that people's lives are affected by the planets and the stars.

astronomer   A person who studies the stars and the other heavenly bodies.

celestial sphere   The dark dome of the night sky, which seems to surround the Earth.

comet   An icy lump that starts to glow when it nears the Sun.

constellation   A pattern of bright stars in the night sky.

heavens   A name for the night sky. Heavenly bodies are the objects that appear in the sky.

meteor   A bright streak made when a speck of rock or metal burns up in the air.

Milky Way   A faint band of light seen arching across the night sky.

nebula   A big cloud of gas and dust in space.

phases of the Moon   The changing shapes of the Moon during the month.

planet   A large body that circles in space around the Sun.

shooting star   A popular name for a meteor.

star   A huge ball of very hot gases, which gives off heat and light.

telescope   An instrument astronomers use to gather light from the stars.

Index